THE MYSTERY SCHOOL
VOL 1

Naomi Navec
Copyright © 2019 Naomi Navec

ISBN: 9781070586618
Imprint: Independently published

CONTENTS

INTRODUCTION

Welcome to the Mystery School.

You've arrived at the beginning of a journey. Not a place with walls or doors or maps but something quieter and harder to define. This is the Mystery School. It isn't somewhere you can travel to, it exists in the space of your own mind, waiting for you to notice it.

The lessons here are not about memorizing facts or chasing perfect answers. They are about learning how to ask better questions.

In truth, the Mystery School is life itself. And life does not come with instructions. Instead, it offers fragments. Moments that almost make sense. Questions that return when everything is quiet. If you have ever stopped and wondered what any of this really means your beliefs, your identity, your existence then you have already stepped inside.

So why question everything? Why not accept what you were told and leave it at that?

Because questioning is how we wake up. It pushes against the limits of what we think we know and loosens the grip of ideas we never chose for ourselves. It is often the first real step toward understanding who you are.

The Purpose of the Mystery School

In this school, there aren't really teachers the way we usually imagine them. Life itself does the teaching. Every experience, the good ones, the painful ones, even the completely ordinary moments, carries something to learn from. The people you meet, the struggles you go through, even the random thoughts that show up in your mind all play a part in that learning. Wisdom is not something someone hands you. It's something you slowly recognize within yourself over time.

Sometimes people worry that questioning everything will leave them feeling lost, like they'll have nothing solid left to stand on. But honestly, the opposite usually happens. When you start questioning things sincerely, you don't lose yourself. You start seeing yourself more clearly. The beliefs you picked up along the way, the expectations others placed on you, the labels you never really chose begin to fall away. And what's left feels steadier, because it actually belongs to you.

And then another realization comes. Life isn't really about finding final answers. It's more about learning how to live with the questions as they grow and change with you. Every question opens something new, not certainty, but understanding. Possibility. When you stop needing everything to be defined, you give yourself room to simply experience life as it is, mysterious, unfinished and alive.

What Can We Gain by Questioning?

There comes a moment when you start questioning the things you always thought were true. And when that happens, something quietly changes inside you. It feels like doors begin opening where there used to be walls. A lot of the fears that hold us back come from beliefs we never really chose. We inherited them, accepted them, and shaped our lives around them without ever stopping to ask why.

But what if some of those beliefs were never true in the first place? What if the limits you feel only exist because no one ever told you that you were allowed to question them?

Questioning things does not mean rejecting everything you believe in. It simply means choosing your beliefs consciously. Seeing them clearly. Understanding what actually belongs to you and what does not. And somewhere along the way, you start noticing life again. The sound of rain against a window. The warmth of sunlight on your skin. Small moments begin to feel meaningful in a way they did before. You know that feeling.

When curiosity takes the lead, life stops feeling like a test you have to pass. It becomes something you explore instead. You realize you are not stuck inside the story you were handed. You can rewrite parts of it. Every assumption you question removes another layer that was never truly yours. What remains feels more real. More honest. It is not about losing yourself. It is about returning to who you have always been.

An Invitation to Begin

This book isn't here to give you answers. It won't tell you what to believe or how you're supposed to think. Its purpose is simpler than that. It's an invitation to look for your own truth.

As you read, there might be moments that feel uncomfortable. Something you always assumed was solid might start to shift a little. That feeling isn't a problem. Most of the time, it means something new is trying to come into view. Stay with it. Let yourself be curious. *What if what you believe is only one part of a much bigger picture? What else might you notice if you allowed yourself to look differently?*

Take a breath for a moment. Slow down. Step into this with an open mind. You don't need to have everything figured out here. There are no rules to follow and no final exam waiting for you at the end. There's only the path unfolding as you walk it.

And this is where it starts.

Welcome to the Mystery School.

Chapter 1

The Illusion of Certainty

Human beings seem to crave certainty. From a young age, we're taught to look for clear answers. We learn what's right and wrong, true and false, real and unreal. Slowly, we build a sense of stability through beliefs, routines, relationships, and the stories we tell ourselves about who we are. Certainty gives us something to hold onto in a world that often feels unpredictable.

But sometimes it's worth asking whether that certainty is actually as solid as it feels. Many of the answers we rely on might simply be stories we learned early on and never thought to question.

The Comfort of Certainty

Certainty feels safe. It makes life seem organized and predictable. It reassures us that we know where we stand and that the ground beneath us won't suddenly disappear. That's part of why humans create systems like religions, governments, philosophies, and scientific frameworks. They help us make sense of things together and give us shared ways of deciding what is true or meaningful.

But certainty has a quieter side too. Once we feel sure about something, we often stop looking beyond it. We hold onto what feels familiar and instinctively resist anything that challenges it. Over time, certainty can begin to limit us without us realizing it. It draws invisible boundaries around what feels acceptable and keeps the unknown safely out of reach.

How Do We Define Truth?

Our need for certainty is deeply connected to our idea of truth. *But what do we actually mean when we say something is true? Is truth something fixed and unchanging? Or is it shaped by experience, perspective, and the way each of us understands the world?*

Think about how differently a child sees life compared to an adult. A child easily finds wonder in ordinary things and believes in possibilities without hesitation. Adults tend to rely more on logic and past experience. Neither perspective is completely wrong. They're simply different ways of seeing.

So does truth change as we grow or do we simply learn new stories about reality?

If truth isn't as fixed as we assume, then certainty becomes less stable too. What feels unquestionable today may one day be reconsidered. History reminds us of this again and again. Ideas once treated as undeniable facts eventually gave way to new understanding. It makes you wonder which of today's certainties might look different in the future.

Certainty as a Form of Control

Certainty doesn't only comfort us. It can also influence us. Because we want clear answers, we tend to trust people or systems that claim to have them. Leaders, institutions, and ideologies often offer certainty through rules, beliefs, or simple explanations. In return, they ask for trust and loyalty.

Religion, politics and even science have all provided powerful ways of understanding the world. Each has helped humanity move forward in different ways. But when any system stops allowing questions, certainty can quietly turn into limitation. Doubt begins to feel dangerous instead of meaningful.

When certainty hardens into something unquestionable, growth slows down. Instead of guiding us, it confines us. Real growth usually begins when we're willing to step beyond what feels completely secure and face uncertainty with curiosity rather than fear.

Can We Live Without Certainty?

The idea of living without certainty can feel uncomfortable. We like knowing where we're going, what to expect, what things mean. Without clear answers, it's easy to wonder how we're supposed to make decisions or feel secure in our lives.

But the truth is, uncertainty has always been there. Nothing is ever completely guaranteed. Not tomorrow. Not success. Not even the things we assume will always stay the same. We just learn to ignore how uncertain life really is because certainty feels safer.

Maybe uncertainty isn't something we need to defeat. Maybe it's something we learn to live alongside. Instead of seeing it as emptiness, we can see it as space. Space to grow, to change, to discover things we didn't expect. Living without certainty doesn't mean drifting without direction. It means allowing curiosity to guide you instead of fear. It means accepting that life unfolds through questions, not final answers.

The Beauty of the Unknown

Certainty can feel comforting, but the unknown carries its own kind of beauty. When we stop needing to understand everything, we make room for wonder again. The vastness of the universe, the complexity of the human mind, the mystery surrounding life and death, these stop being problems to solve and become experiences to sit with.

Some of the most meaningful parts of life exist precisely because we don't know what will happen. Falling in love without knowing where it will lead. Starting something new without guarantees. Holding onto questions that may never be fully answered.

When the need for certainty loosens, life feels different. Less controlled. More alive. Unpredictable, yes, but also full of possibility.

An Invitation to Question

As you reach the end of this chapter, pause for a moment. Think about the things in your life that feel unquestionably true. The beliefs you rarely examine. The ideas you assume are solid.

Have you ever really questioned them? And if you have, what changed afterward? If you haven't, what might happen if you did?

Maybe certainty was never meant to be the destination. Maybe it's one of the most convincing illusions we carry. And maybe, when we loosen our grip on it, we begin to see life with fresh eyes.

This is where the Mystery School truly begins. The first lesson is simple:

Question everything especially what feels impossible to question.

Chapter 2

Who Am I Without My Name?

When someone asks, "Who are you?" the first thing that usually comes to mind is your name. But what does a name really say about you? It is just a label, a sound given to you at the beginning of your life. It helps identify you, but it does not explain who you are. If your name disappeared, along with the roles and labels you have been given, what would be left? Who would you be underneath all of that?

This question goes deeper than it first appears. We spend so much time defining ourselves through our work, our relationships, our beliefs and our achievements that we rarely stop to ask whether these things truly describe us. When everything the world has told you to be is set aside, what remains?

The Masks We Wear

From childhood, we are given names and categories. Daughter or son. Student. Friend. Quiet. Outgoing. Serious. Funny. Over time these descriptions start to feel like identities, shaping how others see us and how we see ourselves.

As life moves on, the roles become more complex. Employee. Partner. Parent. Creator. Success. Failure. Each role carries expectations and little by little we adjust ourselves to fit them.

But are these roles really who we are or are they simply parts we learn to play? Imagine being in a place where no one knew your name, your work or your past. *Who would you be in that moment? Would you feel free or would you feel uncertain about who you are without those familiar definitions?*

The masks we wear can feel comforting. They give us a sense of place and direction. They help us feel that we belong somewhere. But they can also hold us in place. Sometimes we grow attached to an identity long after it has stopped fitting who we are. Change begins to feel threatening, not because we cannot change but because we are afraid of leaving behind the person we think we are.

The Stories We Tell Ourselves

Identity is shaped not only by how others see us but by the stories we repeat to ourselves. We say things like, "I am successful," or "I am not good enough." We tell ourselves that we are our achievements or our failures. These stories begin to feel like facts but they are really interpretations. They are ways of explaining our experiences not the experiences themselves.

Imagine losing everything you usually use to define yourself. Your work, your relationships, your possessions. You would still exist but you might feel as if you no longer knew who you were. This is part of the illusion of identity. We mistake the stories for the self, when the stories are only expressions of something deeper that remains even when everything else changes.

Are We What We Do?

In the world we live in, identity is often connected to what we produce. When we meet someone new, one of the first things we ask is what they do for a living, as if a career could capture the whole of a person.

But what you do is only one part of your life. It raises a quiet question worth sitting with.

Is what you do really who you are?

Imagine a painter who can no longer paint or a teacher who has stepped away from the classroom. *Do they stop being who they are? Or is there something deeper in them that exists beyond those roles?* When we tie our identity to what we do, we risk feeling lost when those roles change, as they always do. A real sense of self cannot depend only on actions or achievements that come and go.

Beyond Societal Definitions

The world around us has its own way of defining people. Names, titles, and labels place us into clear categories that make things easier to understand and organize. These definitions bring order but they rarely capture the full depth of a person.

What happens when we loosen our attachment to those definitions? When we stop thinking of ourselves only as the good daughter, the loyal friend or the hardworking one? What happens when we refuse to be reduced to gender, nationality, or religion alone?

Moving beyond these definitions does not mean rejecting them completely. They can still be useful in everyday life. But they are tools, not truths. They help us navigate the world yet they do not describe the core of who we are.

What Remains When We Strip It All Away?

If you set aside your name, your roles and the labels you carry, what remains? At first, the answer might feel like nothing at all. It can feel like an empty space. But maybe that space is not emptiness. Maybe it is possibility. Maybe the absence of fixed identity is an invitation to rediscover yourself not as a collection of labels, but simply as a living, breathing presence.

Close your eyes for a moment and ask yourself:

Who am I without my name? Without my work? Without my past? Sit with the uncertainty instead of rushing to fill it. In that quiet space, you may begin to sense a part of yourself that exists beyond definitions.

Chapter 3

The Fabric of Belief Systems

Belief systems are woven into human life. They help us make sense of the world, give shape to the unknown, and offer meaning when things feel confusing. Religion speaks about existence, morality and what might come after life. Politics offers ways to organize societies. Science tries to understand reality through observation and testing. All of them promise a kind of clarity. Yet behind that clarity is a deeper question. *Do these systems help us move closer to truth or do they sometimes limit how we see?*

To understand how belief systems shape our reality, we have to look at them carefully. We have to ask what they give us, what they expect from us, and how they influence the way we think and see the world.

The Purpose of Belief Systems

Belief systems come from a very human need to understand what we cannot fully explain. They bring a sense of order to a world that often feels unpredictable. They give people a shared language for understanding life and relating to one another. At their heart belief systems try to answer a few basic questions.

Why are we here?

What is right and wrong?

How should we live together?

What is the nature of reality?

Without some kind of framework, life can feel uncertain and even frightening. Belief systems offer comfort and a sense of direction. They bring people together around shared ideas and values. At the same time, they can also pull people apart. History is full of conflicts between groups who each believed they held the final truth.

The Illusion of Objectivity

Every belief system tends to present itself as the truth. Religions may point to divine revelation. Political movements claim to offer the right path for society. Science relies on careful observation and testing. Yet all of these systems pass through human perception. They are shaped by culture, history and personal perspective.

Science is often seen as the most objective approach, and its methods aim for neutrality. Still, science is carried out by human beings and it changes over time. Ideas that once seemed unquestionable, like the belief that the Earth stood at the center of the universe, were eventually replaced by new understanding. This does not weaken science. It simply reminds us that even our most reliable systems are always evolving toward a clearer picture.

Religion shows the same pattern in a different way. Beliefs that are sacred in one culture may seem unfamiliar or symbolic in another. Political ideas also shift as societies change, reflecting new struggles and new hopes. Each system gives us a way of seeing, but no single way of seeing can reveal everything.

Belief as a Double-Edged Sword

Belief systems can help us understand the world but they can also limit us.

On one side, they bring structure to our thinking and help us make sense of complicated realities. They can inspire progress, creativity, and connection. Scientific curiosity has led to extraordinary discoveries. Religious teachings about compassion have inspired countless acts of care and generosity.

On the other side, belief systems can become restrictive when we hold onto them too tightly. When a belief turns into unquestionable certainty, curiosity begins to fade. Dogma can appear in any system. It insists that the truth has already been found and that there is no reason to keep searching.

A belief system becomes harmful when it demands complete loyalty without room for doubt. It divides people into those who belong and those who do not. Instead of widening our view, it narrows it. Instead of encouraging understanding, it can close the door to it.

How Do We Decide What to Believe?

Choosing what to believe is one of the most personal decisions we make and often one of the most important. Yet most of us never really choose. We inherit beliefs from our families, our culture or the people around us and we carry them forward without stopping to question where they came from or whether they still make sense to us.

To choose our beliefs consciously, we have to ask honest questions. *Does this belief help me grow? Does it deepen my understanding or strengthen my connection with others? Or does it hold me back? Does it close me off from new ways of seeing? And why do I believe it in the first place? Is it something I explored for myself or something I accepted without thinking?*

It is also worth remembering that we do not have to belong to only one way of thinking. Wisdom can come from many places. Science can help us understand the physical world. Spiritual traditions can help us explore the inner one. Social and political ideas can help us shape the world we live in. No system contains everything. Each offers insight, and each has limits.

Living Beyond Belief

What would it mean to live with a little more freedom from belief systems? Not without them but without being confined by them. It would mean approaching life with openness instead of rigid certainty.

Living this way does not require rejecting belief systems altogether. It means recognizing where they help and where they fall short. It means using them as guides rather than treating them as final truths. It means being able to say, this belief makes sense to me right now but I am willing to let it change if I discover something deeper.

This kind of openness allows us to meet life more fully. Instead of clinging to one explanation, we learn to live with complexity. Belief systems become steps along the path rather than walls around us. Each one can bring us closer to an understanding that goes beyond any single framework.

An Invitation to Question

As you reflect on this chapter, think about the belief systems that shape the way you see the world. *Which ones give you strength? Which ones feel restrictive?*

You might ask yourself a few simple questions.

What do I believe about the world and why?

Which beliefs have I never stopped to question?

If I let go of a belief I have always held, would I lose myself or discover something deeper?

Maybe the most meaningful kind of questioning is not about rejecting belief systems completely but about seeing them clearly for what they are. They are human attempts to navigate a mystery that is far larger than any one explanation.

Beyond them is not emptiness. It is an invitation to live, to learn and to keep exploring without reaching the end.

Chapter 4

The Meaning We Chase

What Is the Meaning of Life?

What is the meaning of life? People have been asking that question for as long as we've been able to reflect on our own existence.

Entire religions and philosophies were built around it. On a personal level, most of us search for meaning in love, work, family, achievement or faith. We hope that one day something will make it all make sense. *But what if life doesn't come with a built in meaning? What if meaning isn't something waiting to be discovered, but something we slowly shape ourselves? Would that idea feel freeing, or unsettling?*

Inherent Meaning or Created Meaning

People tend to look at meaning in two main ways. Some believe that life already has a purpose. This view often comes from religious or spiritual traditions, where meaning is seen as part of a larger design. According to this way of thinking, life is not random. There is a direction, even if we do not fully understand it. For many people, this brings a sense of comfort and belonging, like having a place in something bigger than themselves.

Others believe that meaning is something we create. In this view, life does not arrive with a fixed purpose. Meaning comes from the choices we make and the values we hold. Instead of discovering a single answer, we build our own sense of direction. This way of seeing things asks us to take responsibility for the lives we shape and the stories we live by.

Which view is right is not easy to say. Maybe both hold some truth or maybe neither tells the whole story. What is certain is that the way we think about meaning shapes the way we live.

Why We Search for Meaning

Part of our search for meaning comes from knowing that life does not last forever. Human beings are aware of their own mortality and that awareness pushes us to ask why we are here at all. Without some sense of meaning, life can start to feel random or even harsh.

Meaning gives us a way to make sense of things. It helps us endure difficult moments and appreciate the good ones. It gives us a feeling of connection and direction. Still, it is worth asking whether meaning reveals something real about existence or whether it is something we create to calm our deeper fears.

What If Life Has No Fixed Meaning?

The idea that life might not have a built in meaning can feel unsettling. Without a clear purpose, it is easy to wonder what the point of anything is. *Why work toward something? Why love? Why create?*

And yet, that same idea can also feel strangely freeing.

If life does not come with a fixed meaning, then we are free to shape our own. There is no script we have to follow and no final authority deciding our worth. Even small moments can take on depth because we choose to value them. A quiet conversation, a shared laugh, the warmth of sunlight at the end of the day can matter simply because they matter to us.

At the same time, meaninglessness can feel like standing at the edge of something vast and uncertain. If nothing has a guaranteed purpose, then we have to decide for ourselves how to live. That responsibility can feel heavy.

This is the strange tension at the heart of the question. The absence of fixed meaning can feel like both freedom and uncertainty at the same time.

The Stories We Tell Ourselves

Human beings make sense of life through stories. Whether life has a built in meaning or not, we create meaning through the way we understand our experiences.

On a personal level, meaning often comes from the things we care about. Our relationships, our passions, and the hopes we carry for the future become part of the story we tell about our lives. That story gives us direction and a sense that what we do matters.

On a larger scale, societies create shared stories. Religions, traditions and ideologies give people a sense of belonging and a way to understand their place in the world. These collective stories connect us to something beyond ourselves.

But stories are not the same as truth. They are ways of interpreting life, shaped by our experiences and what we long for. Seeing this does not make them meaningless. It simply reminds us that meaning can shift and change over time. It is something alive, not something fixed forever.

Is Meaning in the Journey or the Destination? Many people think of meaning as something to reach, like a final answer waiting at the end of the road. But maybe meaning is not something we arrive at. Maybe it is something we live through.

Think of a traveler moving without a clear destination. At first they might feel lost, unsure of where they are going. But over time, they may begin to notice the richness of the journey itself. The people they meet, the places they see and the things they learn along the way start to matter more than any final point on a map.

Meaning might work the same way. It may not be something we discover once and hold onto forever. It may be something we shape little by little, in the way we live each day.

Living Without Final Answers

What would it mean to live without a clear answer to the question of life's meaning?

One part of it is acceptance. Accepting that life may not come with a universal purpose can open the door to its mystery. Instead of searching for one final explanation, we can learn to live more fully in the present, finding value in the small moments that quietly pass by.

Another part is responsibility. If meaning is not given to us, then it becomes something we help create. That responsibility can feel heavy at times, but it can also be empowering. It means that the shape of a meaningful life is not decided somewhere else. It grows from the choices we make.

When we loosen our need for certainty, space opens up for a sense of wonder. Meaning does not have to be written somewhere far away. It can appear in simple things. The look in someone's eyes when they care about you. A small act of kindness. The quiet feeling of having lived a day honestly.

An Invitation to Reflect

As you finish this chapter, take a moment to reflect.

What gives your life meaning?

Do you feel that meaning is already there, something you discover, or something you create for yourself?

If life had no fixed meaning, how might you choose to live?

Maybe meaning is not a place we arrive at but a question we carry with us. And maybe the act of searching, wondering, and exploring is closer to the meaning of life than any final answer could ever be.

Chapter 5

Time and the Eternal Now

Time

Time is one of those things we live by every day, yet rarely stop to question. We measure it, schedule around it, and feel its pressure constantly. Clocks move forward, days pass and we assume time is a steady force carrying us from the past into the future. *But do we really understand what time is? Is it something that truly exists on its own or is it a way we make sense of life as it unfolds?*

To question time is to question how we experience reality itself. The past, present and future feel separate but maybe they are not as divided as we think. Maybe the only moment we ever truly touch is the one we are living right now.

The Illusion of Time

Time feels solid because we see its effects everywhere. We celebrate birthdays, notice our faces change in the mirror and mark the passing of years through memories and losses. It feels undeniable. Yet science suggests that time may not be as simple as we imagine. It can stretch or shift depending on movement and gravity, which means it is not as fixed as it seems.

Even in everyday life, time behaves strangely. An hour spent with someone you love can disappear almost instantly, while a few minutes of discomfort can feel endless.

This raises a quiet question.

Is time something universal or is part of it shaped by how we experience it?

If time is not as solid as it feels, then maybe what remains is the present moment. The only moment we ever actually live.

Living in the Past

Many people spend a great deal of their lives looking backward. Memories replay in the mind. Old decisions are second guessed. Past experiences become part of the way we define ourselves.

The past can help us understand where we came from, but it can also hold us in place. When we see ourselves only through what has already happened, we limit who we can become. Old wounds and old successes can both keep us from fully being here now.

And yet the past is not a place we can return to. It exists only in memory. When we dwell on it, we are not touching reality itself but a version of it our minds have reconstructed.

Living in the Future

If the past pulls us backward, the future pulls us forward. We plan, hope and worry about what might happen. We imagine better days ahead and work toward them.

But the future, like the past is not something we can step into. It exists only in thought. It is shaped by our expectations, our hopes and our fears. When we live only for what comes next, we place our sense of fulfillment somewhere that never quite arrives.

Too much focus on the future can make us trade the present moment for a promise that may or may not come true. And the present is the only place where life is actually happening.

The Eternal Now

What would it mean to live more fully in the present moment?

To stop being pulled so strongly by the past and the future and return to what is here?

The idea of the eternal now suggests that the present moment is all we ever truly have. The past appears as memory within the present. The future appears as imagination within the present. Everything we experience happens here.

Living in the present does not mean forgetting the past or ignoring the future. The past can guide us and the future can inspire us. But the present is where life unfolds.

How Our Sense of Time Shapes Us

The way we relate to time affects how we live.

When we stay trapped in the past, we may repeat patterns shaped by regret or nostalgia.

When we focus only on the future, we may be driven by fear or endless ambition.

When we return to the present, our actions become clearer and more intentional.

The present is not only where we experience life. It is where we shape it. Every choice we make now becomes part of the past we will remember and the future we will imagine.

The Difficulty of Being Present

Living in the present sounds simple, but it is not easy. The mind is always moving. It revisits old moments and tries to predict what comes next. Staying present takes awareness and practice.

You might ask yourself a few quiet questions. *Can I loosen my grip on what has already happened? Can I release the need to control what has not happened yet? Can I be at ease with simply being here?*

There are no quick answers to these questions but asking them can deepen the way we experience life.

Time as a Tool

Time does not have to feel like something ruling over us. It can be something we use.

The past can teach us without defining us.

The future can guide us without controlling us.

The present is where we are free to act and to live.

When we stop treating time as a master and begin to see it as a tool our relationship with life begins to change.

An Invitation to the Present

Before moving on, pause for a moment. Take a slow breath. Notice the air moving in and out. Pay attention to the feeling of your body where you are sitting or standing. Listen to the sounds around you. Watch your thoughts come and go.

You might ask yourself:

How often do I live in the past or the future?

What would it feel like to live more fully in the present?

Can I find meaning and freedom in what is here right now?

Time keeps moving, but life is always happening here. The present moment is not something you have to search for. It has been with you all along.

Chapter 6

Beyond Duality

From the moment we're born, we learn to see the world in opposites. Good and evil. Right and wrong. Light and dark. These contrasts shape how we understand life. They make things easier to sort out and give us a way to make decisions and judge what we see. But they might not tell the whole story. Maybe reality is more complicated than simple opposites. Maybe the truth sits somewhere beyond them.

To question duality is to step into a space where things don't always fit into neat categories. It's a place where opposites can exist together and where understanding becomes deeper, even if it becomes less simple.

The Comfort of Duality

Thinking in opposites gives us a sense of clarity. It helps us organize the world into something that feels understandable. We rely on these distinctions when we ask ourselves basic questions.

What is good and what is evil?

What is true and what is false?

What counts as success and what counts as failure?

These lines give us direction. Without them, the world might feel confusing and unstable. Duality creates the feeling that there is order even when things are uncertain.

The Limits of Opposites

But while duality makes life easier to understand, it can also oversimplify it. When we divide everything into opposites, we often miss what lies in between.

Are actions ever completely good or completely evil, or do they depend on intention and circumstance? What one culture calls right, another might call wrong. Even light and darkness depend on each other. One only makes sense because of the other.

Sometimes we create clear divisions where life is actually continuous. Reality is not always split into separate pieces. Often it is more like a spectrum.

What Exists Between Opposites

The space between opposites is often where deeper understanding begins. Between good and evil, right and wrong, light and dark, there are countless shades that reflect the complexity of being human. In that middle space, opposites stop looking like enemies and start looking more like parts of the same whole.

> Compassion and justice can seem opposed, yet real balance needs both. Too much forgiveness without accountability creates problems but so does punishment without understanding.

Chaos and order work the same way. Too much chaos creates instability but too much order can make life rigid and lifeless. Life seems to unfold somewhere between the two.

Even life and death, which appear to be complete opposites, are deeply connected. The fact that life ends is part of what gives it meaning, and every living thing carries that ending within it from the start.

When we stop forcing ourselves to pick one side or the other, we begin to see more clearly.

Moving Beyond Duality

Moving beyond duality does not mean throwing it away. Opposites can still help us navigate everyday life. They help us make choices and understand consequences. The problem comes when we believe reality must always fit into simple either or categories.

Going beyond duality means being willing to hold contradictions without rushing to resolve them. It means recognizing that things that appear opposite can still belong together. Strength and vulnerability, for example, often grow side by side.

It also means loosening our need to judge everything as good or bad and asking instead what each experience might teach us. Beyond strict opposites is a way of seeing where everything is connected. The divisions start to soften, and reality feels less like separate parts and more like a moving whole.

The Role of Duality in Growth

Seeing the world in black and white can be a starting point. It helps us form values and make decisions. But as we grow, we often begin to see that things are more complicated than they first appeared.

Instead of asking whether we are right or wrong, we might start asking what we can learn. Instead of labeling people as good or bad, we might try to understand their perspective.

Growth often means moving from simple answers toward a more layered understanding of life.

The Dance of Opposites

You might think of opposites as partners rather than enemies. Light and darkness define each other. Success gains meaning through failure. One gives shape to the other.

Instead of being locked in conflict, opposites move together in a kind of balance. Life seems to unfold through that movement.

Seeing this can change how we approach the world. Instead of constantly choosing sides, we start noticing how different forces work together to create the whole.

An Invitation to Reflect

As you sit with these ideas, think about the opposites that shape the way you see your life.

What divisions do you rely on the most?

Where have you reduced something complex into a simple choice between two sides?

What might change if you explored what exists in between?

Beyond opposites is a way of seeing that feels more fluid and complete. It does not reject differences, but it looks beneath them for what connects everything together.

The next time you face an either or choice, pause for a moment and ask what might exist beyond those two options. You might find that the answer is wider than you expected.

Chapter 7

The Paradox of Free Will

Free Will

Free will is one of those ideas most of us hold onto without thinking twice. We like to believe we are choosing our own path, making decisions for ourselves, shaping our lives according to what we want. It feels natural to think of ourselves as being in control. But if you look a little closer, the picture becomes less clear. How free are we, really? And how much of what we do is influenced by things we never chose in the first place?

Our biology, the way we were raised, the culture around us, even simple chance all play a role in the choices we make. If so much is already shaping us behind the scenes, what does freedom really mean? And if we are not completely in control, could accepting that bring a kind of quiet relief instead of fear?

What Is Free Will?

Free will is usually described as the ability to choose for ourselves. The idea is that, when faced with a decision, we are free to pick our own direction.

But that raises a few uncomfortable questions. *Why do so many of our decisions feel automatic? Why do we fall into habits we did not consciously choose? How much of what we call a choice is actually influenced by things like our upbringing, personality, or environment?*

It is possible that we hold onto the idea of free will partly because the alternative feels unsettling. The thought that we might not be fully in control is hard to accept.

To explore this idea honestly, we have to look at some of the forces that shape us without us noticing.

The Forces That Shape Us

Part of what we do comes from biology. Our brains are wired in certain ways that influence how we react and make decisions. Studies suggest that sometimes the brain begins forming a decision before we are even aware of it. Genetics also shape us more than we like to admit, influencing temperament, tendencies, and emotional patterns. It raises the question of how much freedom we really have if part of the script is already written into us.

Society also plays a powerful role. From the beginning of our lives, we absorb expectations about how to behave and what to value. We learn what success looks like and what is considered acceptable. It is worth wondering how many of our desires are truly our own and how many were quietly shaped by the world around us.

Then there is circumstance. None of us chooses the time or place we are born into. Opportunities and limitations often depend on factors we never controlled. Some people describe this as fate, while others simply call it chance. Either way, it reminds us that our lives unfold within conditions we did not create.

Do We Really Choose?

If free will exists, then we are the authors of what we do. Yet many of our reactions feel almost automatic. People lose their temper even when they promised themselves they would stay calm. Old habits return even when we try to leave them behind. Certain patterns repeat, sometimes without us fully understanding why.

This suggests that much of what we do is influenced by forces operating beneath the surface. Even the decisions we make consciously are shaped by past experiences, emotions and surroundings.

That does not necessarily mean free will is an illusion. It might simply mean that freedom grows with awareness. The more we understand the forces shaping us, the more room we may have to choose differently.

If Not Us, Then What?

If we are not fully in control, then what is guiding our choices?

Part of the answer may lie in the unconscious mind. Hidden fears and desires influence us more than we realize. Becoming aware of them can give us more clarity and a stronger sense of direction.

Another part lies in the fact that we are connected to other people. Our lives unfold within relationships and systems that shape us in ways we cannot always see. Recognizing that connection can help us make more thoughtful decisions.

Some traditions suggest a different way of looking at freedom altogether. Instead of trying to control everything, they speak about moving with the flow of life. In that view, freedom is less about forcing outcomes and more about living in alignment with something larger than ourselves.

The Paradox of Free Will

Free will sits in a strange tension. We want to feel in control, yet so much of life is unpredictable. The harder we try to control everything, the more we notice how much remains outside our reach.

Maybe freedom is not only about control. Maybe it also involves acceptance. Maybe peace comes not from mastering life but from learning to live with its uncertainty.

Surrender as Freedom

The word surrender can sound like defeat, but it can also mean something quieter and stronger. Letting go of the need to control every outcome can open a different kind of freedom.

Surrender does not mean doing nothing. It means recognizing what we can change and what we cannot. It means acting with intention while accepting that life will never be completely predictable.

When we stop fighting every influence and every uncertainty, we sometimes discover a deeper freedom. Not freedom from all limits, but freedom to live within them with awareness.

Can Letting Go Bring Peace?

Strangely enough, peace often grows when we accept that control has limits.

When we stop trying to manage everything, we can focus on what truly matters. When we release the need to control the future, the present becomes clearer. When we allow life to remain partly mysterious, it becomes easier to live with what is.

An Invitation to Reflect

As you sit with these ideas, think about your own sense of choice.

Do you feel in control of your decisions?

What influences the way you act and respond?

What might change if you stopped trying to control everything and allowed life to unfold a little more naturally?

Maybe free will is not about controlling life completely. Maybe it is about choosing how we respond to what life brings. And maybe, in that space of response, something like freedom begins to appear.

Chapter 8

The Void and Creation

The Void

The void is one of those ideas that pulls in two directions at once. It can feel unsettling, even frightening, and yet strangely intriguing. We tend to imagine it as emptiness, a kind of endless nothing where there is no meaning and no light. But at the same time, the void is often where things begin. Before a thought takes shape, before something new comes into existence, there is a kind of open space where it all starts.

So what is the void, really? Is it emptiness in the sense of loss and disappearance or is it more like a beginning that hasn't taken form yet? Can something truly come out of nothing or is the idea of nothingness itself something we misunderstand?

To think about the void is to face some of the deepest questions about existence, and sometimes the answers are not what we expect.

What Is the Void?

Most of the time we picture the void as pure absence. No substance, no meaning, no direction. It feels like the opposite of being alive. Like a blank canvas before anything is painted on it. Like silence before a sound is made. Like an empty page before the first word appears.

But emptiness does not always mean nothing. Even what we call empty space is not truly empty. There is movement and energy even where nothing seems to exist. What looks like nothing can still hold possibility.

On a more personal level, the void often appears in moments of change. It is the quiet after something ends. The stillness after a dream falls apart. The pause before something new begins. It can feel like standing in an empty space, but that space often turns out to be where the next chapter starts.

Can Something Come From Nothing?

People have wondered for centuries whether something can come out of nothing. The question shows up in science and philosophy and even in everyday life.

When we think about the universe, there is still a mystery about how everything began. Somehow, what we see today came out of a state we can barely imagine. However we explain it, existence itself suggests that beginnings can emerge from what looks like emptiness.

The same thing happens on a smaller scale in creative work. A writer begins with a blank page. An artist begins with an empty surface. An idea appears where, a moment before, there was nothing clear or defined. It feels as if something grows out of an open space.

Maybe the void is not truly empty at all. Maybe it holds the possibility for things that have not yet taken form. Like a pause before movement or darkness before the first light of morning.

The Fear of Emptiness

For many people, the void feels threatening. It represents the unknown and the loss of structure. It raises the possibility that life might not come with built in meaning, and that thought can be difficult to face. It forces us to confront the idea that what we build and love may not last forever.

But maybe the void is not only about loss. It can also be part of change. Many spiritual traditions speak of emptiness not as a lack but as a state where things are free to take new shape. Instead of seeing emptiness as an end, they see it as a beginning.

The void becomes frightening mostly when we resist it. When we allow it to be what it is, it often reveals itself as a space where something new can grow.

The Void and Creation

Every act of creation seems to begin with a moment of nothing. A pause. A silence. A space where nothing is clear yet.

An artist faces an empty canvas and feels uncertain where to begin but that same emptiness allows imagination to move. A writer sits in front of a blank page, unsure what to say and slowly an idea takes shape. A patch of bare ground may look lifeless, yet it holds the possibility of growth waiting beneath the surface.

The void is not necessarily an ending. Often it is the ground where creation begins.

Fear or Acceptance

It is natural to fear the void. The unknown always carries a certain unease. But the void is also part of how life moves forward.

We encounter it during transitions. When something ends before something else begins. When familiar structures fall away. These moments can feel empty, yet they often open the door to change.

In creative work, the void is the starting point. In life, it reminds us that nothing stays fixed forever. Everything moves between fullness and emptiness.

When we stop pushing the void away, it begins to look different. Instead of pure absence, it starts to feel like possibility.

An Invitation to Reflect

Take a moment to think about your own experiences with emptiness.

Have there been times when everything felt uncertain or empty?

What came out of those moments? Did they lead only to loss, or did something new begin to take shape?

What would it mean to accept the void as part of life instead of something to avoid?

The void is not simply the absence of life. It can be the space where life begins again. To stand in that space is to face the unknown and to realize that what looks like nothing may actually be the beginning of everything.

Chapter 9

The Mirror of Relationships

Relationships as Mirrors

Relationships are woven into every part of being human. Through other people we learn, grow, and sometimes struggle. They shape the way we see the world and the way we see ourselves. But maybe the people in our lives are more than just companions or strangers we happen to meet. Maybe they also reflect parts of us that we might not notice on our own. Every connection, every moment of love, even every disagreement might hold something for us to understand.

When we look at others, we assume we are seeing them clearly. But often what we see is mixed with our own fears, hopes and expectations. In many ways, getting to know others is also a way of getting to know ourselves.

Do We See Others Clearly?

When we meet someone, it feels natural to think we are seeing them as they really are. We notice what they say and how they act and we form opinions. But our perception is never completely neutral. We interpret people through our own experiences and assumptions.

Sometimes we project our own feelings onto others without realizing it. If we feel insecure, we might read judgment into someone's silence when there is none.

Other times we place people on a pedestal, seeing in them qualities we wish we had ourselves.

In that sense, relationships can act like mirrors. The things we admire or dislike in others often point back to something within us. Someone's confidence might inspire us because it reflects a strength we want to develop or it might bother us because it touches on our own doubts.

Through others, parts of ourselves become visible.

The Lessons in Conflict

Conflict is usually something people try to avoid but it can reveal a lot. When we clash with someone, we are often facing our own reactions and sensitivities as much as the other person.

Many disagreements grow out of feeling misunderstood or unheard. We react strongly when something touches a deeper need or wound. In those moments, conflict shows us what matters to us and where our limits are.

It can also push us to look at things from another point of view. When we take time to understand the other person's perspective, even if we do not agree, something opens. We begin to see the situation more fully.

Handled with awareness, conflict does not have to break relationships. Sometimes it strengthens them. It shows us where we can grow and where we need to be more honest with ourselves.

The Lessons in Love

Love, in all its forms, changes us. It asks us to open up, to trust and to let ourselves be seen as we are.

Romantic love often touches our deepest hopes and fears. It invites closeness but it also reveals our patterns. We might notice how we seek reassurance or how we pull away when things feel too intense. Love shows both our strengths and our wounds.

Friendships and family bonds bring a different kind of closeness. They give us a sense of belonging and support but they also reflect the beliefs we carry about ourselves and about others.

And underneath all of this is the way we relate to ourselves. The way we treat ourselves often shows up in the way we treat the people around us. When we are harsh with ourselves, it becomes harder to be gentle with others. When we learn to accept ourselves our relationships often become more open and steady.

Connection and Shared Humanity

At a deeper level, relationships remind us that we are not as separate as we sometimes think. Every person we meet is living their own story, facing their own struggles and hopes. Seeing that can soften the boundaries between "me" and "them."

When we approach relationships with curiosity instead of certainty, something shifts. We begin to ask quieter questions.

What might this person be showing me about myself?

What might I learn if I look beyond their words and actions?

What happens if I stay open, even when it feels uncomfortable?

Seen this way, every interaction has something to offer.

What Relationships Can Teach Us

Relationships are not only about companionship or disagreement. They are also about growth.

Through conflict we learn patience, self awareness and the importance of boundaries.

Through love we learn vulnerability, forgiveness and connection.

Through everyday encounters we learn presence and empathy, remembering that everyone we meet carries unseen experiences.

Even brief encounters can leave something behind if we pay attention.

An Invitation to Reflect

Take a moment to think about the people in your life.

Who challenges you the most, and what might that be showing you about yourself?

Who inspires you, and what does that reveal about who you could become?

How might your relationships change if you saw them less as separations and more as reflections?

The mirror of relationships is not always comfortable to look into, but it can show us things we might never see on our own. When we begin to understand this, we may notice that every relationship, whether joyful or difficult, carries something of value. Through others, we slowly come to understand ourselves.

Chapter 10

Beyond the Mind

Beyond the Mind

The mind is one of our greatest strengths. It helps us understand things, solve problems, and make sense of a world that can feel confusing at times. Without it, we wouldn't be able to plan, learn or create anything meaningful. But as helpful as the mind is, it can also make things harder than they need to be. It keeps thinking, questioning and trying to explain everything. Sometimes it holds on too tightly to needing answers and creates stories about who we should be or how life is supposed to unfold.

Maybe the mind isn't meant to have the final say. There's another kind of understanding within us that doesn't come only from logic. When we move beyond constant thinking, we begin to notice intuition, emotions, and those quiet inner feelings we often ignore. Some of our most honest realizations don't come from overthinking, but from simply feeling and listening to what's already there.

The Mind as a Tool

The thinking mind is powerful. It helps us understand the world and solve practical problems. It's behind science, invention, philosophy and art. It helps us adapt and move forward.

At the same time, the mind can work against us when it never switches off. Too much thinking can turn into overthinking, where the same thoughts circle again and again without leading anywhere. The mind can fixate on imagined problems and worst case scenarios, feeding anxiety instead of clarity. It can also build identities and beliefs that separate us from others or from parts of ourselves we don't fully understand.

The mind works best when it's used as a tool, not when it runs the whole show.

When the Mind Becomes a Trap

One of the mind's strongest habits is trying to stay in control. It wants clear answers and solid ground. It sorts the world into categories so everything feels manageable. That can help but it can also limit us.

The mind tends to prefer simple either or thinking instead of complexity. It pulls us back into old memories or pushes us forward into imagined futures, often at the expense of what is happening right now. It clings to what feels familiar and hesitates in front of the unknown even when change might lead somewhere better.

In trying to control life, the mind sometimes forgets how to simply experience it.

The Quiet Voice of Intuition

There is another kind of knowing that appears when the mind grows quieter. Intuition often shows up as a subtle sense of direction that doesn't come with a full explanation. It might feel like a quiet certainty, a sudden insight, or a simple sense that something is right or wrong.

Because intuition cannot be easily measured or explained, it is often dismissed. Yet people have relied on it for as long as we have been human. It seems to gather information in ways the thinking mind cannot always follow.

Sometimes intuition appears as a gut feeling or a sudden clarity. Other times it shows up as a creative spark that comes out of nowhere. Many discoveries and creative breakthroughs began with an intuitive leap before logic caught up.

Emotion and the Hidden Mind

Much of who we are lies outside of conscious thought. Beneath the surface, emotions and memories shape our reactions and choices in ways we don't always notice.

Emotions are often treated as problems to manage, but they can also be signals. They tell us something about what matters to us and what affects us deeply. Listening to emotions instead of pushing them away can open the door to a deeper kind of understanding.

The subconscious mind holds patterns and memories that influence us quietly. Dreams, symbols, and sudden insights often rise from this deeper layer.

Paying attention to them can reveal things that ordinary thinking misses.

When we begin to include emotion and the subconscious in our awareness, our understanding becomes wider than logic alone can provide.

Tool or Trap

The mind is both a tool and a trap, depending on how we relate to it. The key is balance. The mind serves us well when we use it to understand, plan, and solve problems. It helps us make sense of the outer world.

It becomes limiting when it tries to control everything and leaves no space for intuition, feeling or presence. When the mind insists on certainty in every situation, it can close us off from experiences that cannot be neatly explained.

Moving Beyond the Mind

Going beyond the mind does not mean rejecting it. It means allowing other parts of ourselves to have a voice too.

Sometimes that means trusting a quiet feeling when a decision has to be made. Sometimes it means allowing emotions to be felt instead of pushed aside. Sometimes it means paying attention to patterns in our dreams or recurring experiences in our lives.

And sometimes it simply means being still for a moment and letting the noise of thought settle. In that stillness, something deeper often becomes easier to hear.

Intuition and Logic Together

Intuition and logic don't have to compete. They work best together. Logic helps us understand how things work. Intuition often points us toward why something matters.

Logic works within what is already known. Intuition moves more easily into what is still uncertain. When the two come together, they give a fuller picture than either one alone.

An Invitation to Reflect

Take a moment to think about your own relationship with your mind.

Do you depend mostly on analysis and logic?

How often do you listen to your intuition or pay attention to your feelings?

What might you notice if you allowed your mind to grow quiet for a while?

Beyond the constant activity of thought, there is another kind of understanding waiting to be noticed. Exploring it doesn't mean leaving the mind behind. It means going beyond its limits and discovering a wider sense of who you are.

Chapter 11

The Sacred Mystery

The Sacred Mystery

Mystery is woven into life. It's there in the vastness of the universe, in the depths of our own inner lives and in the questions that never quite settle into clear answers. People have always tried to understand the big mysteries. *Why are we here? What is reality, really? What happens when life ends?* Every time we find an answer, it seems to open the door to more questions.

Maybe mystery is not something we are meant to solve completely. Maybe it's something we learn to live with. Instead of being an obstacle, it might be what gives life its sense of depth and wonder. It may not be the answers that make life meaningful, but the act of searching and asking in the first place.

What Does "Sacred" Mean?

When people hear the word sacred, they often think of religion, rituals or holy places. But the sacred isn't limited to religion. It's that quiet sense of reverence you feel when something touches you deeply. It's the feeling that there is something greater than yourself, even if you can't explain what it is.

You might feel it watching a sunrise or listening to a piece of music that moves you for no clear reason. It might appear in a quiet moment alone or in something as simple as hearing a child laugh. Sometimes it shows up when you look at the night sky and realize how vast everything is, or when you notice the beauty in something small and ordinary.

Seeing mystery as sacred means approaching life with humility and curiosity. It means accepting that some things may always remain beyond our understanding and recognizing that this isn't a failure. It may actually be part of what makes life meaningful.

Are Mysteries Meant to Be Solved?

Human beings naturally want answers. We like to understand how things work and to turn the unknown into something clear. That drive has led to incredible discoveries and has changed the way we live.

But some questions seem to stay just out of reach. People still wonder what came before the universe began. We still don't fully understand how consciousness arises from the brain. Even ideas like infinity stretch the limits of what we can truly grasp.

Some mysteries may never have final answers. And maybe they don't need to. Sometimes the mystery itself is enough. It gives us something to wonder about and reminds us how vast existence really is.

Living With Mystery

Living with mystery means accepting that we cannot know everything. It means letting go of the need to have every answer and allowing uncertainty to be part of life.

There's a kind of humility in that. It reminds us that we are small parts of something much larger than we can fully understand.

At the same time, mystery keeps curiosity alive. It invites us to explore, to question and to imagine. Without mystery, life would lose much of its sense of possibility.

And when we stop demanding clear answers for everything, something else becomes possible. We begin to feel a quiet sense of wonder simply from being here at all.

Awe and Wonder

Awe and wonder are not just emotions. They are ways of looking at the world.

A moment of awe can shift how we see things. It can make us feel connected to something larger than our individual lives. For a moment, the usual boundaries soften, and we sense that we are part of something bigger.

Wonder brings a different kind of energy. It keeps curiosity alive and makes space for imagination. It allows us to approach life with openness, even when things are uncertain.

Some truths are not meant to be measured or explained. They are meant to be experienced.

Mystery and Meaning

Mystery doesn't take meaning away from life. In many ways, it gives life its depth. The fact that we don't know everything leaves room for discovery and surprise.

Imagine a world where every mystery had already been solved. Every question answered, every outcome predictable. It might be orderly, but it would also feel empty. Without the unknown, much of what inspires us would disappear.

Mystery invites us to find beauty in unanswered questions. It encourages us to discover meaning in the act of exploring rather than in reaching a final answer. Life begins to feel less like a problem to solve and more like a story that keeps unfolding.

An Invitation to Reflect

Think for a moment about the mysteries in your own life.

What questions have stayed with you over the years?

Are there things you once tried to solve that you might now be willing to simply live with?

What might change if you met the unknown with curiosity instead of resistance?

Mystery is not something broken that needs fixing. It is something to live with. To honor mystery is to step into life as it is, vast and unfinished, and to recognize that not knowing can be part of what makes the journey meaningful.

Chapter 12

Liberation Through Questioning

The Power of Questions

Questions open doors. Most of us started asking them as kids. *Why is the sky blue? Why do things happen the way they do?* That curiosity is how we begin to understand the world. But somewhere along the way, many of us are taught to stop asking. We're encouraged to accept what we're told and treat it as settled truth. It can feel safer that way. Certainty gives a sense of order. But it can also box us in without us noticing.

Maybe questioning everything isn't something to be afraid of. Maybe it's a way of becoming freer. When we loosen our grip on fixed answers, we sometimes discover a deeper connection to ourselves and to the world around us. Questions can help us peel away beliefs we never chose and see things with clearer eyes.

The Courage to Question

It takes courage to question what you think you know. When you question something deeply held, the ground can feel less steady. If one belief turns out to be wrong, it raises the uneasy thought that other things might be uncertain too. That can feel uncomfortable, even frightening. People like to feel in control, and questions can make life feel less predictable.

But questions are also how we grow. They clear out ideas that no longer fit and make space for new ways of seeing. They keep curiosity alive and stop us from becoming rigid. And sometimes the most important thing a question reveals isn't about the world. It's about ourselves.

To question is to step outside the comfort of certainty and into the possibility of change.

Letting Go of Answers

We're trained to look for answers. In school, at work, and in everyday life, knowing the right answer is usually rewarded. It feels good to solve something and close the book on it. But sometimes that sense of closure is misleading.

Answers can make us think we've reached the end of the road, when in reality the road keeps going. Life doesn't stay still and neither do the truths we live by. An answer that feels solid today might turn into a new question later on.

There is a strange freedom in admitting that you don't have everything figured out. When you stop needing final answers, the pressure eases. Instead of forcing certainty, you can settle into the process of exploring and learning as you go.

Letting go of answers doesn't mean rejecting knowledge. It means recognizing that discovery is ongoing.

How Questions Change Us

Questions have a way of changing things, sometimes quietly and sometimes all at once.

When we question our beliefs, we begin to see which ones truly belong to us and which ones we simply inherited. Some beliefs fall away and others take their place in a way that feels more honest.

In relationships, questions can deepen understanding. Asking why we react the way we do or what we really expect from others can reveal patterns we didn't notice before. Questions make space for empathy and for seeing beyond surface disagreements.

And when we turn questions inward, they can lead to deeper self understanding. Asking who we are, what we value and why we live the way we do can bring us closer to something real. Each question becomes a step toward seeing more clearly.

Peace in Not Knowing

Questioning is often seen as unsettling, but it can also bring a quiet kind of peace. When you no longer feel the need to have all the answers, something relaxes inside you.

Uncertainty stops feeling like an enemy and starts feeling like part of being alive. Life becomes less about reaching a final point of certainty and more about staying open to what unfolds.

There can even be joy in that openness. Questions keep us curious and present. They keep life feeling alive and unfinished in the best way.

When you trust that life doesn't have to be fully explained, it becomes easier to move with it instead of constantly trying to pin it down.

The Freedom in Questioning

Questioning can be deeply freeing.It frees you from beliefs that no longer make sense to you. It frees you from the pressure to know everything. It gives you room to explore and change.

Questioning doesn't mean tearing everything apart. It means widening your understanding. It means moving through life with open eyes and an open mind.

An Invitation to Reflect

Think for a moment about the role questions play in your life.

What beliefs have you never really questioned?

What might change if you stopped needing certainty all the time?

How would it feel to see questioning not as doubt, but as a way forward?

Freedom isn't found in having every answer. It grows from the willingness to explore and to stay curious. The deepest truths in life rarely arrive as neat conclusions. More often, they appear through the questions we're brave enough to ask.

Chapter 13

The Mystery of Life and Death

Life and Death

Life and death may be the deepest mysteries we ever face. They are tied together so closely, yet we tend to see them as complete opposites. Life is something we celebrate. Death is something we fear. Life feels like presence, while death feels like absence. But maybe they are not truly opposites. Maybe they are parts of the same larger movement, stages in something far bigger than we can fully understand.

To think about life and death is to face the unknown in its most direct form. The questions they raise may never be fully answered, yet they can change the way we live, the way we love and the way we face what is inevitable.

What Is Life?

Life is both obvious and mysterious at the same time. We see it everywhere. In a heartbeat, in a growing plant, in the laughter of a child. It feels real and immediate, yet the deeper we look, the harder it becomes to explain.

Science can describe how life works. It can explain cells, genes, and the conditions that allow living things to exist. But it still leaves open the deeper question of why life exists at all. *What is it that turns matter into something alive? Is life simply the result of chance or does it come from something deeper that we do not fully understand?*

Then there is consciousness. Life is not just movement and biology. It is also awareness. Somehow the physical brain gives rise to thoughts, feelings and experience. No one fully understands how that happens. It leaves open the question of whether we are only physical beings or whether there is something more at work within us.

The more we look at life, the more mysterious it seems.

What Is Death?

If life is mysterious, death is even more so. It is the one certainty every living being shares, yet it remains unknown until it happens.

People have always wondered whether death is an ending or a kind of transition. Some believe it is simply the end of existence, a return to nothing. Others believe it leads into another form of being, whether that means an afterlife, rebirth, or some kind of merging with something greater.

It is possible that death might be both an ending and a beginning at the same time. The closing of one chapter and the opening of another.

Much of the fear around death comes from not knowing what follows. But it also comes from what death takes away. The people we love, the identity we built, the life that feels familiar. Accepting death means facing the reality that everything we know is temporary.

And yet, it is often the awareness of death that gives life its depth. Knowing that time is limited can make moments feel more meaningful. It can remind us to pay attention, to care more deeply, and to appreciate what we might otherwise overlook.

The Cycle of Life and Death

Many traditions see life and death as parts of a continuous cycle rather than separate events. One gives way to the other, and then back again.

Nature shows this clearly. Leaves fall and decay, and from that decay new growth appears. Winter gives way to spring. What looks like an ending often becomes a beginning in another form.

A fallen tree returns to the earth and feeds new life. In that sense, death is not simply disappearance. It is transformation.

Maybe existence itself moves in cycles we cannot fully see. Maybe life and death are not separate at all but different expressions of the same unfolding process.

Finding Peace in the Mystery

Accepting the mystery of life and death means accepting that some questions may never have clear answers. But that acceptance can bring a kind of peace.

When we stop trying to outrun death, we can focus more fully on living. Each moment becomes more precious when we realize it will not last forever. Part of life's beauty comes from the fact that it passes.

Recognizing the mystery of death also deepens our sense of life. The two belong together. One gives meaning to the other.

Like the rising and setting of the sun, life moves in rhythms larger than us. Even if we do not understand what lies beyond, we are still part of something vast and ongoing.

An Invitation to Reflect

Take a moment to think about your own relationship with life and death.

What does life mean to you?

How does knowing that life ends shape the way you live?

Is it possible to feel at peace with not having all the answers?

Life and death may not be enemies after all. They may be partners in the same unfolding story. Together they form the rhythm of existence, inviting us to live fully, to love deeply, and to accept the mystery that surrounds us.

Maybe the deepest truth is that life and death are not separate at all. And in seeing them as part of the same whole, something inside us begins to relax.

Chapter 14

The Tapestry of Religions

Religion

Religion is one of the oldest ways human beings have tried to understand life. Across different times and cultures, people have turned to faith, rituals and stories to make sense of the big questions. *Where do we come from? Why do we suffer? How should we live? What happens after we die?* Religion has offered ways to find meaning and feel connected to something greater. At the same time, it has also created divisions and sometimes been used to control or exclude.

Looking at religion honestly means seeing both sides. There is wisdom in it but also complexity. It reflects something deeply human. The desire to understand life and to feel part of something bigger than ourselves.

What Is Religion?

At its heart, religion is a response to the unknown. It gives structure and meaning to a world that can often feel confusing.

Religion tries to answer questions about where we came from and why we are here. It offers moral guidance about how to live and how to treat others. It brings people together through shared traditions and rituals. And for many, it offers a way to feel connected to something beyond ordinary life, whether that is described as God, spirit, or ultimate truth.

Even though religions differ, many of them share similar themes. Stories of creation appear again and again. So do ideas of good and evil, struggle and transformation. These similarities suggest a common human longing to find meaning beyond everyday life.

The Beauty in Religion

Religion has inspired some of the most meaningful things people have created. Works of art, music, architecture and philosophy have often grown out of spiritual traditions.

Sacred teachings from different traditions speak about compassion, humility, and the search for truth in ways that still resonate today. Rituals such as prayer, meditation, or gathering with others can bring a sense of peace and connection. For many people, religion is not only belief but also community. It provides a place where people support one another and share a sense of belonging.

At its best, religion encourages people to reach toward love, kindness and unity.

The Difficult Side of Religion

Religion has also had a more complicated role. The same beliefs that unite people can also separate them.

When religious ideas become rigid, questioning can be discouraged. Dogma can make it difficult to explore new perspectives or think freely. At times, religion has also been used as a way to gain power, with leaders using belief to influence or control others.

History shows how religious differences have sometimes led to conflict. When people believe their tradition holds the only truth, it can create divisions and intolerance.

Fear of doubt can also become a barrier. Yet without questioning, it is difficult for understanding to deepen.

Questioning Without Rejecting

Questioning religion does not always mean turning away from it. Sometimes questioning is a way of searching more honestly.

It can help us recognize what still feels meaningful and what no longer does. Some teachings, like compassion or respect for life, feel universal no matter where they come from. Some practices bring a genuine sense of meaning, even if we do not accept every belief that surrounds them.

At the same time, we may let go of ideas rooted in fear or exclusion. We may come to accept that not everything needs a final explanation.

Religion can be seen not as a fixed set of answers, but as a path that continues to evolve.

Spirituality Beyond Religion

For some people, spirituality becomes a more personal way of exploring the sacred. Instead of following a single tradition, they draw from different sources and focus on direct experience.

Spirituality often emphasizes personal reflection, meditation or quiet awareness. It allows people to explore meaning in their own way without needing to fit into a defined system.

This shift does not necessarily reject religion. It reflects an ongoing search for connection and meaning that goes beyond labels.

An Invitation to Reflect

Think about the role religion or spirituality has played in your life.

What parts of it feel meaningful to you?

What parts raise questions?

How do you experience the sacred in your own way?

At its core, religion is one way human beings try to engage with the mystery of existence. Its forms may differ, but the intention is often the same. To find meaning, to feel connected and to move closer to truth.

When we allow space for both reverence and questioning, our understanding of the sacred can grow deeper.

Conclusion: The Journey Continues

Reaching the end of this book is not really an ending. If anything, it's the beginning of something ongoing. The questions explored here are not meant to be settled once and for all. They are meant to stay with you, to return at different moments in your life in new ways.

Life itself is a kind of mystery school. Its lessons come through experience more than through clear answers. Every moment, whether joyful or difficult, has something to teach if we are willing to pay attention.

The Role of Questions

Questions are not problems to eliminate. They keep us awake and curious. Every time you question your beliefs, your identity, or your purpose, you open the door to change.

Questions like these may stay with you:

Who am I beneath the roles I carry?

Is meaning something I discover or something I create?

What happens when I let go of certainty?

Can I live more fully in the present?

These are not riddles to solve. They are companions for the road ahead. The answers may shift over time, but the act of questioning keeps leading you forward.

Life as a Mystery School

If life is a mystery school, then every experience is part of the learning. There is no final point where everything is understood. No moment when the journey is complete. And maybe that is part of what makes it meaningful.

This path does not promise certainty. Instead, it invites you to live with uncertainty and find meaning within it. Growth is less about becoming someone new and more about uncovering what was already there beneath everything you were taught to believe.

Living the Questions

The poet Rainer Maria Rilke once suggested that we try to live the questions instead of rushing toward answers. There is wisdom in that idea.

When you live with questions:

You stop feeling pressured to have everything figured out. You stay open to new ways of seeing.

You begin to realize that the journey itself has value.

An Invitation Forward

As you close this book, carry the questions with you.

What beliefs might you look at more closely?

What uncertainties might you learn to accept?

How might you live more fully right where you are?

The path ahead belongs to you. It may not always be clear, but it will be alive and changing. And that may be exactly what makes it worth walking.

Chapter 15

Knowledge and Power

Knowledge and Power

Knowledge is often seen as a kind of power. It helps us understand what's happening around us, make choices, and shape the direction of our lives. From ancient teachings to modern science and technology, the search for knowledge has changed the course of history and opened doors that once seemed impossible to reach. But knowledge doesn't come without responsibility. The same understanding that can help people grow can also be used to influence or control.

Looking at knowledge and power together means asking how we use what we learn, who gets access to it, and whether there are limits to what should be known. People often say knowledge sets us free and sometimes it does. But knowledge can also create pressure, division or dependence. The real question may be how we carry it and what we choose to do with it.

What Knowledge Really Is

Knowledge is more than collecting facts. It's what happens when information begins to make sense and becomes something we can use in real life.

Some knowledge is practical. These are the skills that help us function in the world, the things we learn through experience and repetition. Other knowledge is more abstract. It helps us understand ideas and patterns that aren't always visible. And then there is the kind of knowledge that comes from within. Self awareness, intuition and emotional understanding often guide us just as much as anything we learn in books.

Knowing something gives us the ability to act with intention. It helps us solve problems and move forward with more clarity. It also gives us a sense that we can influence our own path, even when things are uncertain.

When Knowledge Becomes Power

People often say that knowledge is power because understanding gives us influence. It allows us to shape our surroundings and sometimes even the decisions of others.

Knowledge can be deeply empowering. It allows people to question what they've been told and imagine new possibilities. Education has lifted people out of difficult circumstances and helped reshape entire societies.

But knowledge can also be used in the opposite way. Those who control information often hold influence over others. Throughout history, knowledge has sometimes been kept in the hands of a few or shaped to support those already in power. The question of who has access to knowledge and who does not still matters today.

The Responsibility That Comes With Knowing

Knowledge itself isn't good or bad. What matters is how it's used.

Many discoveries have improved lives in incredible ways, from medicine to technology. At the same time, knowledge has also been used to build tools of destruction or to spread misinformation. The same information that can educate people can also be used to manipulate them.

This raises difficult questions. *Are there things we should be careful about discovering or sharing? Should some knowledge be limited because of the harm it might cause?* Curiosity pushes us forward but responsibility asks us to move carefully.

The Limits of Knowledge

For all its value, knowledge has limits. It keeps changing as new discoveries appear and old assumptions fall away.

Sometimes knowledge creates the illusion that we have things figured out. But the more we learn, the more we realize how much remains unknown. Wisdom often begins with that recognition.

There may also be things that remain beyond human understanding. Just as there are limits to what we can see or hear, there may be limits to what we can fully know. Accepting that doesn't weaken knowledge. It gives it perspective.

Knowledge and Wisdom

Knowledge and power are closely connected but power without wisdom can lead in the wrong direction. Knowledge works best when it's guided by something deeper.

That means using what we learn not only for ourselves but in ways that benefit others too. It means remembering that knowledge is a tool, not the final goal. And it means staying curious while also staying humble, knowing that every answer leads to new questions.

Sharing Knowledge

In a world shaped more and more by information, access to knowledge matters more than ever.

When education and information are shared widely, people have more opportunity to grow and contribute. Knowledge expands when it's exchanged and discussed. It becomes richer when different perspectives are allowed to meet.

Seeing knowledge as something to share rather than something to guard helps it reach its full potential.

An Invitation to Reflect

Take a moment to think about your own relationship with knowledge.

How do you use what you know? Does it help you grow, or does it sometimes limit you?

Are you willing to question your own understanding, or do you hold onto certainty?

How might you use knowledge in a way that benefits not only yourself but others as well?

Knowledge is a gift but it's also a responsibility. Used with care and awareness, it can change lives and shape the world in meaningful ways.

In the end, knowledge may not be about collecting answers as much as deepening our understanding. Sometimes wisdom means knowing when to search, when to act, and when to accept that some things will remain a mystery.

A Closing Thought

Life may not be about reaching final answers at all. It may be about learning to live with the questions. Mystery isn't a problem that needs fixing. It's something to experience.

To walk this path is to stay open to the unknown, to remain curious, and to accept that life holds more possibilities than we can ever fully grasp.

Your path is your own, but you're not the only one walking it. Every question you ask connects you to others who are searching in their own way. We're all learning as we go, one question at a time.

Thank you for walking this part of the journey. May your curiosity stay alive and may your questions keep leading you forward.

To be continued...

About The Author

Naomi Navec is a multifaceted writer with a passion for exploring mental health and relatable life topics. She began her journey in storytelling at the age of 10, writing her first movie script and participating in theatrical performances during her school years. Her early involvement in public plays across different schools laid the foundation for her creative projects.

In addition to her work in screenwriting, Naomi has written several books that explore themes such as hope, healing, and personal development. Among her notable works are **Mystery School** and A **Book to Give You Hope** (Healing Words of Hope), which offer readers reflection and inspiration drawn from her own experiences and observations.

Naomi's commitment to mental health awareness is clearly reflected in her writing, where she approaches complex emotions and the human experience with empathy and understanding. Through her books and screenplays, she aims to inspire and encourage, offering readers tools and perspectives to better navigate life's challenges.

Beyond her literary work, Naomi is active on social media, where she shares her thoughts and connects with a wider audience. Her Linktree provides access to her Instagram, Facebook, and other online resources, allowing followers to discover her work and join her community, "Born To Inspire."

Naomi Navec's passion for storytelling and mental health continues to deeply resonate with readers and audiences, establishing her as an important voice in conversations surrounding emotional well-being and personal growth. Through her work, she builds a bridge between raw human experiences and meaningful dialogue, encouraging others to embrace their struggles and find healing throughout their journey.

www.ingramcontent.com/pod-product-compliance
Lightning Source LLC
Chambersburg PA
CBHW051431280526
45785CB00003B/1239